Hope Springs

— POETRY FOR THE SOUL —

VOLUME 2

Ana Lisa de Jong

LANG
BOOK PUBLISHING

LANG
BOOK PUBLISHING

langbookpublishing.com

National Library of New Zealand Cataloguing-in-Publication Data

Lang Book Publishing Limited 2015

Scripture quotations are taken from THE HOLY BIBLE, NEW INTERNATIONAL VERSION®, NIV® Copyright © 1973, 1978, 1984, 2011 by Biblica, Inc.® Used by permission. All rights reserved worldwide.

ISBN 978-0-9941292-0-8 – Paperback
ISBN 978-0-9941292-2-2 – Hard Cover
eISBN 978-0-9941292-1-5 – eBook
eISBN 978-0-9941292-3-9 – ePub

Published in New Zealand
A catalogue record for this book is available from the National Library of New Zealand.
Kei te pātengi raraunga o Te Puna Mātauranga o Aotearoa te whakarārangi o tēnei pukapuka.

To my husband always
whose home is in my heart,
and whose heart is my home

Poetry Is

Poetry is

Flying without wings.
Uplift without a breath of wind.
Dancing on the air
while still firmly on our feet.

Yes Poetry is

The gift to put to music
the images that come.
Weaving words to give them life
and movement of their own.

Oh Poetry is

Insight and observation.
A longing to crystallise
into permanence,
rhyme and reason for it all.

Except Poetry is

The ability to see things afresh,
to understand the nuances
and on the shifting carpet
dance.

So Poetry is

Conflict at the core.
As joys and sorrows surge
we rise and we fall.
At the mercy of time's passage,

while in the current standing still.

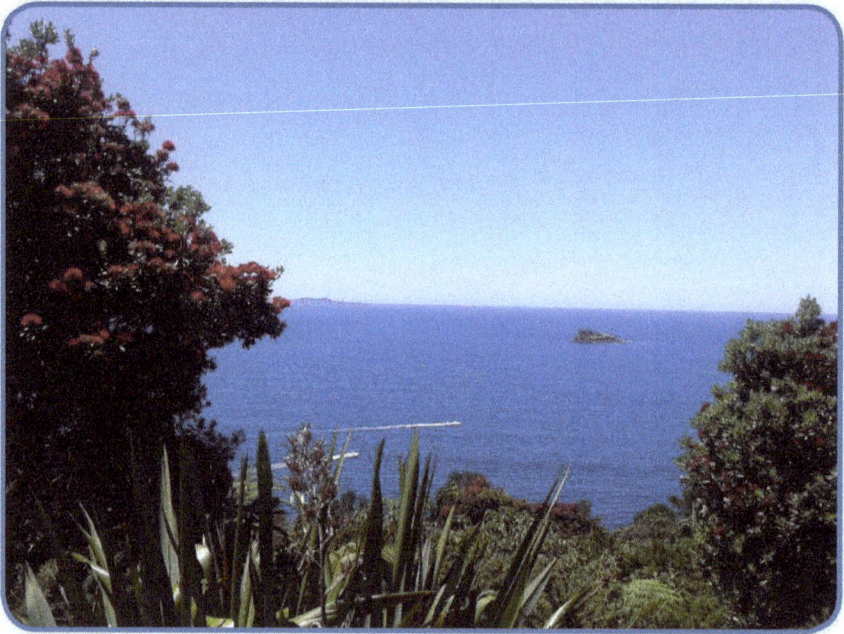

Contents

PART 3: LOVE

Foreword

A few years ago I made my first trip to London, a city that I had always dreamed of visiting. Because of my love for art high on the list of things to do was to visit the National Gallery and the National Portrait Gallery. For years I had only ever interacted with many of the great works of art through books and magazines, and finally I was able to see the originals. There is something very surreal about standing before one of these great works of art. In many ways it is overwhelming to the senses. Engaging with art in this way is a spiritual experience, with each work speaking differently to all those who encounter it. More than that, however, is the fact that every time we encounter a piece of art we will see different things, encounter different things, notice different things.

The great Greek historian, biographer and essayist Plutarch once said that *'painting is silent poetry, and poetry is painting that speaks'*. This small volume of poetry has come from the heart as a gift to the world. Contained in its pages are a myriad of paintings. Some are great works of art with large subjects, bright colours and bold brush strokes. Others are much smaller, more delicate and subtle. And yet each piece will speak in unique ways. Each piece will touch the reader in unique ways.

Ana Lisa de Jong would never call herself a master painter, she is too humble for that - and yet she is. This volume attests to her skill and the depth of her talent. Building on her earlier work *Songs in the Night*, this new volume *Hope Springs* takes the reader on a wonderful new journey.

From the simplicity of *Thankful* to the depth and wonder of *Sunset*. Each piece is a unique work of art that truly speaks to the soul; paintings that speak to the very depth of who we are. In these pages the casual reader will encounter bright colours and picturesque scenes, whereas the more seasoned traveller will find a depth of palette found only in the great masterpieces of the world. And through it all, every reader will discover one resounding thing, the presence of God. His fingerprints can be seen in each work, for His spirit inspires the author. As the first poem in this anthology suggests faith comes quietly. To any who venture beyond the opening page, they will encounter a faith as vibrant and deep as the poems which articulate it.

This collection is a gift. A gift to the soul. A collection of paintings that we can all return to over and over again and be captivated, inspired, encouraged, comforted, blessed.

Chaplain Class 1, Colonel Lance Lukin, OSTJ, QHC.
Principal Defence Chaplain
New Zealand Defence Force

Introduction

As I write this Introduction, I reflect on the journey to wholeness I am walking right now. A journey back to myself. If life is indeed a circle, with its seasons, and its joys and struggles; nothing happens in isolation, our present being influenced by each step we have journeyed up to now.

Recently I felt God direct me to the bible verse, *'see, I am doing a new thing! Now it springs up; do you not perceive it? I am making a way in the wilderness, and streams in the wasteland'* (Isaiah 43:19, NIV). I looked carefully for the evidence of 'new creation' in my life, as to all appearances my peace and joy had taken leave, and my resilience was crumbling. In time though I registered the truth of German poet Bertolt Brecht's quote, *'crisis takes place when the old has not yet died, and the new has not yet been born'*.

Unexpectedly laid low, I felt God comfort and minister to me, as the beautiful verse in Hosea attests to, *'therefore I am now going to allure her, I will lead her into the wilderness and speak tenderly to her. There I will give her back her vineyards, and will make the valley of Achor a door of hope.'* Today as I write this I feel I have gained new insight about the depth of His love and compassion for us, His commitment to our growth and wholeness, even though at times His work in us may be painful. It is my prayer that you will be reminded afresh by the poetry contained in this book, of this enduring message of hope, which is God's love, and faithful heart towards us.

Although much of the poetry in this book is reflective of the inner work God has been doing in my heart over this past year, I consider what poet Cecil Day Lewis said, that *'we do not write in order to be understood; we write in order to understand'*. Without the 'dark' contained in these poems, there would not be the opportunity to thread through the 'light'; the message of faith, which is always hope and love. This message of faith acknowledges and affirms 'who' we are, and 'where' we are right now, while continuing to extend hope out to us. Always with the hopeful 'but'. Yes, we mourn but He will, '...*comfort all who mourn, and provide for those who grieve in Zion... bestow on them a crown of beauty instead of ashes, the oil of joy, instead of mourning, and a garment of praise, instead of a spirit of despair...'* (Isaiah 61:2-3). Yes, it may be dark right now, but '...*rejoicing comes in the morning.'* (Psalm 30:5, NIV).

We may be let down by others, or our own failings, and the knocks of life, but when we are let down it is into the very arms of God, who will lift us up. We are buoyed up by the *'hope that springs eternal'* (Alexander Pope). We are confident that, '...*He who began a good work in you (us) will carry it on to completion...'* (Philippians 1:6, NIV).

Faith, hope and love, these three things remain. They always have been, and always will be. We will have trouble, *'but take heart! I have overcome the world'* (John 16:33, NIV). But for faith, hope and love, what do we have and what do we keep? But, in the end they are everything, and all we ever need for Him to do His complete work in us.

Lately, I have been thinking of the promise, *'and if I go and prepare a place for you, I will come back and take you to be with me that you may also be where I am.'* (John 14:3, NIV). This 'place', I believe, is not only our promised residence in heaven, but a promise we can claim right now. A rest deep down in our soul. An assurance of safety, security and joy, no matter who we are, and no matter our journey thus far, or our journey to come. It is a message for us all, without exception.

Go well.

Ana Lisa de Jong
Living Tree Poetry

'We did not come to remain whole. We came
to lose our leaves like the trees.
The trees that are broken. And start again,
drawing up on great roots.'
ROBERT BLY, FROM 'A HOME IN DARK GRASS'

'But blessed is the one who trusts in the LORD,
whose confidence is in Him.
They will be like a tree planted by the water
that sends out its roots by the stream.
It does not fear when heat comes;
its leaves are always green.
It has no worries in a year of drought
and never fails to bear fruit.'
JEREMIAH 17:7-8 (NIV)

Part 1:

FAITH

*'Faith is the bird that feels the light and
sings when the dawn is still dark.'*

RABINDRANATH TAGORE

Faith Comes Quietly

Faith comes quietly.
So quietly you would almost swear, it were not there,
but gone somewhere, never to return, again.
At least not now, while you're in,
this well of despair.

But faith comes quietly.
The faith you thought stole out with the night,
was only shrouded from view, with your focus on the dark.
And as your head, sunk low with grief, began to lift,
it slipped back in to view.

Faith comes quietly.
Never believe what your doubts state to be true,
only believe what faith tells you to.
For only by believing can you receive, only by believing will you see,
the fruits of faith at work in your heart.

Faith comes quietly.
Resilient, flexible, it bends like a bow in the storm.
Faithful, unshakeable, it remains, though we,
may be picked up and blown to the ground.
Until we find that faith, our encourager and uplifter,

is our quiet, sturdy backbone.

'The Lord is close to the broken–hearted
and saves those who are crushed in spirit.'
PSALM 34:18 (NIV)

Light and Dark

Black and white
Light and dark
Pain and pleasure
Night and day

What is one without the other?
Passion requires the boundaries of sanity.
Reality needs the possibilities of imagination.
Feelings need thoughts to give them shape.
Thoughts need feelings to give them depth.

Joy and sorrow
Young and old
Sun and moon
Lost and found

What is life but a dance?
From one foot to another, balancing.
Like the seasons, life needs its ebb and flow.
The solemn reflection after pleasure fleeting,
and the joy that rises continually.

Near and far
Empty and full
Sweet and bitter
Hot and cold

What is light without the dark?
What is depth without height's comparison?
After intimacy comes the necessary withdraw.
From ecstasy's heights we must always fall.
And yet as night draws in we can anticipate the dawn.

Life and death
Heaven and earth
Future and past
Faith and disbelief

Where-ever we are, close or far,
to where we want to be, we know we won't remain there.
Though shifting shadows move to block out the sun,
by its very nature light will keep shining.
And whether we believe it or not,
life, after winter's apparent death, emerges again.

'God called the light day, and the darkness He called night.
And there was evening and there was morning, one day.'
GENESIS 1:5 (NIV)

Peace

Let me go.
Let go of me.
Let me run far from here.
To a place where I am not necessary.
Where I can be alone,
without expectations.
Without the frustrations,
of being here.
Of being everything to all of you,
of being continually emptied.

Let me go.
Let me go,
to a place where I can fill.
Where I can renew and restore.
Where life instead of taking,
gives to me,
more than what it draws.
Where I can breathe and stretch.
Retreat from the world and reconnect.
Not with you all, but with my soul.

There is a voice,
that's calling me softly.
I don't know from where,
though it's not from here.
But from where there's no noisy needs,
to harass me.
Only peace to shore up
my fragile defences;
and calm,
to soothe my shattered senses.

Let me go.
Let go of me.
It only takes a moment to steal away,
and breathe.
To look up at the sky, so still and calm.
To listen to the birds,
and the rustling leaves.
To feel the cool evening air,
on my cheek.
To become aware of a gentle presence.

For peace is not found if we run away.
Perhaps for a moment,
but it soon dissipates.
Peace is found when we release our burden.
When we accept ourselves,
and realise our boundaries.
When we feel,
the weight of the world on our shoulders,
yet call on Him, from where we stand,
to restore us.

For His peace
is not something we must find,
or run to obtain.
But something we receive,
in our weakness,
and in our dependence, claim.
And if I close my eyes for a moment,
and draw breath.
Peace will come softly,
as sure as His promises.

'I have told you these things, so that in Me you
may have peace. In this world you will have trouble.
But take heart! I have overcome the world.'
JOHN 16:33 (NIV)

Hidden in Him

You are hidden close in Him,
and His life is in you.
His greatness contained in your small frame.
Your life guarded, and in His hand enclosed.

Who would you be, if you could truly believe,
if you could comprehend, what you held inside?
Would you recognise His heart beat in time with yours?
Would you feel, coming like a flood, the fullness of His life?

Who would you be, if you could truly understand,
that He treasures you, like His most dear and precious find?
Each one of us imperfect, fragile, but hemmed in near.
Each one of us, the much desired, much loved, apple of His eye.

You are hidden from shame, sheltered far from pain,
and the unkind glare of a fallen world.
In every need, your defender comes to your aid,
and guarded by His wings, you are kept shielded and secure.

Who is He who both keeps us, and is kept by us?
Who is He who both infuses and envelops us?
If we could allow Him to penetrate, and fill us,
would we then understand that His plan for us is 'one-ness'?

A return to the Creator, who is both our source and maker.
A return to the home from whence we came.
Back to Him, from whom our DNA originated,
the author of each and every one of our cells.

What does it feel like for us to come home?
To know His life in us, and know by Him our lives are held.
To truly believe there is a haven from our fears,
a retreat to safety, and a God who wants us near.

It feels, it feels like finally knowing.
Knowing we are hidden close, at home with Him.
Knowing that His life is inscribed within.
His greatness contained in our small frame,
and we in His hands encompassed.

'Keep me as the apple of Your eye, hide me
in the shadow of Your wings...'
PSALM 17:8 (NIV)

Thankful

Thankfulness
It's the only way we can live with life.
It's the only cover for the chill of the night.
It's the only light to ward off the dark.
It's the only way to hold close, that which without,

thankfulness and gratitude,
might dissipate.

Thankfulness
It's the only way we can find salvation.
It's the only way we keep from drowning.
It's the lifeline we need to keep us upright.
It's the only way that we can obtain,

faith and assurance
of our hopes not failing.

Thankfulness
It's our only key to peace in suffering.
It's our only comfort when losses bear down.
It's our only joy, when joy's hard to find.
It's the only way to still ourselves enough,

to see, there is still treasure left
in an open palm.

'Every good and perfect gift is from above, coming
down from the Father of the heavenly lights, who
does not change like shifting shadows.'
JAMES 1:17 (NIV)

Longing I Come

Longing I come.
Not to be sated of my thirst,
but to find the deeper yearning,
that lies underneath.
To be understood.
To be fully accepted.
To be affirmed.
To know a deeper connection.
Than this world offers,
with its temporary relief.
To know what it is to no longer thirst.
To be free from the bondage of needs.

But as I journey further,
my longings lengthen as shadows on a summer's evening.
Just as my shadow is always a step ahead,
so with His spirit, or how does He lead?
The longing behind my yearning,
is not meant to be sated in full.
I have not arrived when I'm truly satisfied,
my holiness is not dependent on contentment.

Contentment speaks of needs being fully met,
or accepting what I have; where I'm at.
While my longing heart knows there's more of Him to know.
So much more to receive, when I truly acknowledge my need.

A journey that's never over.

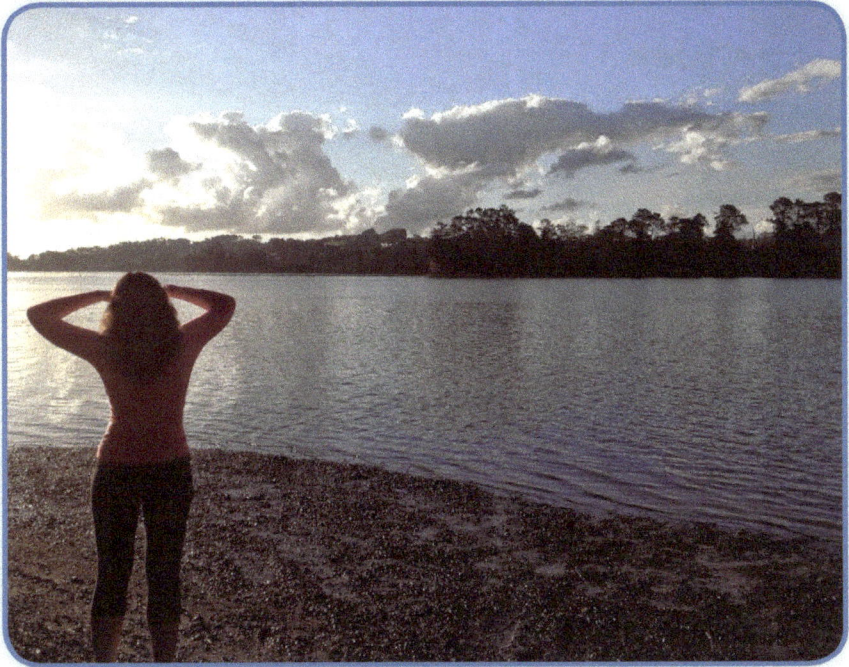

'My soul thirsts for God, for the living God.
When can I go and meet with God?'
PSALM 42:2 (NIV)

Punishment

I can't leave,
this pew.
On my knees facing You.
Head bowed,
praying humility
will restore my
broken pride.

As standing here
cooking tea;
I pretend
to be present,
when in truth,
I'm far away.
Chasing You.

Head down,
chastised,
on my broken knees.
As in my mind,
I exert punishment
less than kind,
and undeserved.

But we do,
don't we?
We make ourselves our own enemies.
And then we sit in the dark,
shutters drawn in.
Wishing the sun
would shine again.

So I don't want to leave,
this place.
Until You come
stained glass shining,
to tell me that I can stand.
As what I've done
is contained in Your hand.

My foolish fears
of what might come,
You absorb in Your mercy.
As the sun might
dry tears upon my skin.
Reminding me again,
love wins.

So I stand here,
cooking tea.
Realising that You've
come to me.
The place I ran to,
hard pew in the dark,
thinking was just punishment

was condemnation, disguised as conviction.
Which long ago, You saved us from.

'I, even I, am He who blots out your transgressions,
for My own sake, and remembers your sins no more.'

ISAIAH 43:25 (NIV)

The River

Broken

I float, adrift, anchorless,
unable to fight the current, or choose direction.
Powerless, and unresisting.
A piece of driftwood,
fallen from the branch.
At the mercy of the river,
and the direction of the current.

Alone

Frail heart grieving.
Defenceless
in the water's wake.
No defeating feeling with reason,
or options to choose from.
Instead, surrender to the rivers pace,
the only choice remaining.

Helpless

Yet, aren't we all defenceless
in the light of God's might?
Our attempts to stand our ground,
so feeble in His sight.
When circumstances dictate
we rest in His arms,
we only fight in vain, helplessly flailing.

But afloat.

Which simply reminds us
that we're held too tight to resist.
We long for arms around us,
and forget we're already in His grip.
Afloat on His river of mercy, His current of life.
And we're to journey with Him
where-ever the river takes us.

'…you whom I have upheld since your birth,
and have carried since you were born.
Even to your old age and gray hairs I am He,
I am He who will sustain you.
I have made you and I will carry you;
I will sustain you and I will rescue you.'
ISAIAH 46:3-4 (NIV)

Something New

You make something new every day.
You, oh God of sunrises,
birdsong and bursting shoots;
spiders webs, dew drops and opening buds.
And though we wake,
and breathe the new breath given to us;
offered like nectar in a cup from God,
we close our eyes to the gift, and re-assume our cast off selves.

And yet, if He can create something new
and astounding in the dark;
as daffodils and sea foam left by the departing tide,
what more can He do, with us? Hearts burdened by our thoughts.
What can He do with a heart
open to His touch?
What can He do? Once we remember to recognise,
He comes, bearing new life.

Not just once, and not just for this precious earth.
But in each breath, and ultimately for us.

'Praise the Lord, my soul;
all my inmost being, praise His holy name.
Praise the Lord, my soul,
and forget not all His benefits—
who forgives all your sins
and heals all your diseases,
who redeems your life from the pit
and crowns you with love and compassion,
who satisfies your desires with good things
so that your youth is renewed like the eagle's.'

PSALM 103:1-5 (NIV)

Part 2:

HOPE

'Hope springs eternal in the human breast;
Man never is, but always to be blessed:
The soul, uneasy and confined from home,
Rests and expatiates in a life to come.'

ALEXANDER POPE,
FROM 'AN ESSAY ON MAN'

Sunset

The clouds.
I watch them change.
From pink to purple, to yellow, to silver.
And I notice that,
whatever their hue,
though they may change to grey,
and reflect the sombre shade,
of my heart.
I still see the blue,
behind them still.

And the blue.
The blue remains.
Though the winds blow,
and the clouds skim,
across a sky forever,
in a state of change.
The blue stays true.
Showing us that it's what's behind,
not the forefront,
which we must hang on to.

Our feelings,
simply an artist's palette.
Every shade of light and dark,
shifting across our days and nights;
determining our view,
shaping our lives.

But even when the sun sets
and darkness draws in cold,
the blue returns when morning dawns,
although it were never gone.

'To Him who alone does great wonders. His love endures forever.
Who by His understanding made the heavens. His love endures
forever. Who spread out the earth upon the waters. His love
endures forever. Who made the great lights. His love endures
forever. The sun to govern the day. His love endures forever. The
moon and stars to govern the night. His love endures forever.'
PSALM 136:4-9 (NIV)

Arms of Grace

I think of You saviour,
with arms unfurled.
Nails driven deep,
in hands holding the world.

I think of You saviour,
a spear in Your side.
Wounded for our transgressions,
Your life ebbing as the tide.

Fingers curled in pain,
tears of blood on the ground.
Light of the world snuffed out,
with hardly a sound.

I think of You Saviour,
scars borne for me.
A life exchanged for life,
captive to set me free.

I think of You saviour,
embracing us on that cross.
Your arms outstretched,
to draw close to You the lost.

As we couldn't save ourselves,
You took it on Yourself.
Never let me forget saviour,
the cup of sacrifice.

I think of You Lord Jesus,
seated at God's right hand.
The veil torn in two,
the victory obtained.

I think of You Lord Jesus,
what Your pain achieved for me.
To worship You forever,
to fall down on bended knee.

Only to have You lift my chin, and
put Your scarred hands in mine.
Embrace me with Your arms of grace,
enfold me in eternal life.

'For to this you have been called, because Christ also suffered
for you, leaving you an example, so that you might follow
in His steps. He committed no sin, neither was deceit found
in His mouth. When He was reviled, He did not revile in
return; when He suffered, He did not threaten, but continued
entrusting Himself to Him who judges justly. He Himself bore
our sins in His body on the tree, that we might die to sin and
live to righteousness. By His wounds you have been healed.
For you were straying like sheep, but have now returned to the
Shepherd and Overseer of your souls.'

1 PETER 2:21-25 (NIV)

In Your Light

My tears, from where You sit
are not simply translucent on my cheeks;
but rather coloured in Your sight,
in every hue of rainbow light.

My mess, from where You sit,
the fruitless striving and backwards steps;
appear to sew a pattern of mistakes,
until You turn the tapestry on its back.

And in wonder, I see

My life, from where You sit,
is not all fumbled stitching and fraying threads,
but rather beauty designed with loving intent,
by an artist who weaves together frailty and strength.

My future, from where You sit,
is not coloured by error, but marked out by potential.
The tears that I shed not wasted and hopeless,
but refined and polished to a silver thread.

And I see

Reflected in Your light, the 'light' of who I am -
when my life, and its despair;
all its brokenness and tears,
is beheld by You through the eyes of grace.

'But we have this treasure in jars of clay to show that this all-surpassing power is from God and not from us. We are hard pressed on every side, but not crushed; perplexed, but not in despair; persecuted, but not abandoned; struck down, but not destroyed. We always carry around in our body the death of Jesus, so that the life of Jesus may also be revealed in our body.'

2 CORINTHIANS 4:7-10 (NIV)

In The Mirror

"You say I surprise you with My gifts,
encouragement at the moment it's needed,
insight to your heart's deepest thoughts,
comfort laid directly on the hurting parts.
'How did you know?', I feel you say,
'how did you know God that I was caught?
Caught up in the web of my own making,
spiralling down with doubts'.

But is anything beyond My knowledge my daughter?
Is anything a surprise to My Spirit?
If you knew the extent that I lived in you,
and how much My love surrounds;
you would not doubt My devotion for a moment,
and would never for a moment feel alone.
So look in the mirror and when you see the image of yourself,
see Me too, for we are not separate, but bound.

And each concern of yours is a concern of Mine.
Each doubt in yourself, I will find, and remind you,
that you are made in the image of Me, and
because of that you are rich in possibility.
There is no measure you can use to define yourself,
that can capture the potential I have placed in you.
You must only believe that when you don't feel enough
I, with you, My body, make a multitude.

You say I surprise you with My gifts,
but you to Me are My prize.
And just as I've graced you with My presence,
you grace the world by being the you that I have designed.
Don't question any more, but explore,
see who you are, all its wonders and its flaws,
but please do not deride what you find,
for you are worth so much more than you recognise."

'Yet the Lord longs to be gracious to you;
He rises to show you compassion.'
ISAIAH 30:18 (NIV)

To Lose

Why are we so afraid to lose?
To surrender back to Him what has always been His.
Is it because we think we will not care in this certain way again?

Or is it that we're afraid there will be a day,
that we no longer remember our lost possessions?
And it will then be clear, that it was only for a season.

And why are we so desperate to hold on to a season?
As though summer won't write words of love once more on our skin.
As though winter won't bring us its silent offerings, as treasures in the
darkness.

As though joy won't cause our heart to skip a beat
as spring breaks us open,
and we respond and soften as a child, with pure expectation.

Why are we afraid to lose?
When we must lose to gain.
While each season's gifts are spent, and running out like rain, through
our hands

a new day's waiting in the wings.

*'A person's days are determined; You have
decreed the number of his months
and have set limits he cannot exceed.'*

JOB 14:5 (NIV)

Inside

I like to live inside myself.
I make it beautiful there.
I take the dirty washing and make it clean.
I take the shambles and the stumbles
and I put them into order;
learn how to walk purposefully again.

I like to live inside myself,
where I talk to myself in words;
and in pictures.
Remembering beauty is always present,
and love is running through,
our lives like a river runs, constant and true.

I like to live inside myself.
I find there's always someone there.
I find my truest, clearest self,
who answers back to me,
with words that take me by surprise,
with their sense and clarity.

I like to live inside myself.
It's a wondrous place to be.
So great in capacity
as to contain all,
the beauty of this earth.
All my loves, and my discoveries,
held in memory

for perpetuity.

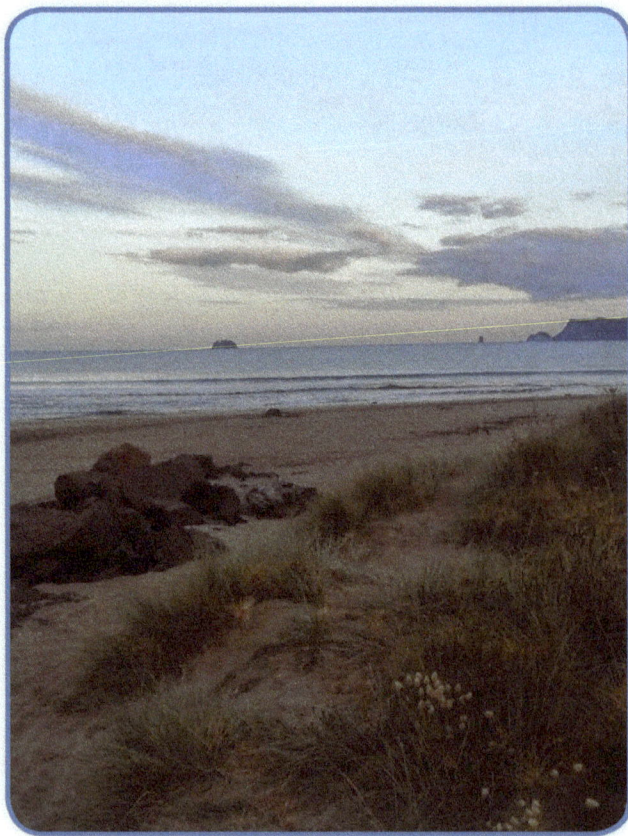

'The Lord will guide you always; He will satisfy
your needs…You will be like a well-watered garden,
like a spring whose waters never fail.'
ISAIAH 58:11 (NIV)

Wings

What does moving on mean?
What do we take with us?
And what do we leave behind?

Is it seeing clearer,
from what has brought us joy and pain?
As the sky is washed clean, by the departing rain.

Do we break the shackles,
that hold us fast in place?
And how do we do that, while cherishing what's been?

How do we move on,
not knowing what lies ahead?
What is the assurance it's better, that it will replace our treasure here?

So we stand pulled in two directions.
Knowing that time, like gravity,
is a law we may begrudge, but cannot escape.

And that what we carry with us
will determine the weight of our load.
So how, how on earth do we give up, what will weigh us down?

We must find a way,
to use the lessons of the past.
To allow the memories to enrich us, as the blood in our veins.

To discard shame for our wrongs,
and welcome forgiveness in.
Knowing that acceptance is the key to moving on.

That while we rail against reality,
we stand with two feet apart.
Hanging in limbo between the future and past.

That the present is all we ever have.
The present and its forward momentum,
takes with us all of our treasure, what we've turned to gain.

So how do we move on?
By recognising the past is necessary.
Colouring the blank canvas ahead, it's a backdrop to all that will be.

We don't have to extricate ourselves.
Everything that's been said, and done, right or wrong;
can, if held lightly, give us wings.

'Forget the former things; do not dwell on the
past. See, I am doing a new thing!
Now it springs up; do you not perceive it?'
ISAIAH 43:18 (NIV)

54

Where There is Injury

'Where there is injury, pardon',
St Francis said.

Did he know how hard it is, to truly forgive?
Is it from experience that he spoke to us these words?
Or is it an ideal, too high for us to fully achieve?

And is it possible, I ask myself,
when the ones we must forgive, continue in their ways?

'Where there is hatred, love'.
Love from where?

When the well is empty,
when rebuffs make a sham of our best intents,
when we've spent ourselves on ungrateful hearts.

How do we find resources to give again,
without recompense?

'Where there is despair, hope.'
Perhaps there is nothing that,

we can do to change the lens they look through,
and ultimately how we too are viewed.
But we can choose, to see ourselves in the light of grace,

and let hope remind us of the truth,
that in His view, we are good enough.

'Where there is darkness, light.'
Perhaps the hardest to perceive.

For what if the darkness we see,
that wells up and floods our minds,
is not actually in others, but in us all the time?

Perhaps the gift of the dark,
is to have light shine upon, the areas we've been blind.

'Where there is sadness, joy.'
Perhaps that's the trick to our salvation?

The injuries we need pardoned; the love we need to cover over all our sins;
the hope to show us the way forward, into the light,
that darkness, our old friend, keeps hidden…

Is to give ourselves (though we may crucify ourselves),
permission, to be our own consolation.

'He was oppressed and afflicted, yet He did not open His mouth;
He was led like a lamb to the slaughter,
and as a sheep before its shearers is silent,
so He did not open His mouth.'
ISAIAH 53:7 (NIV)

Let the Night Fall

Let the night fall.

Let it come and rest,
soft as a blanket
over the mistakes of our day.
With its absolving hand,
let it wipe away -
the missteps,
the regrets,
the disappointments.
The offences we've received,
and in our weakness, made.
But which in their injustice
burden,
and relentlessly shake,
our tender frames.

Let the night fall.

Let it come
and restore
all we failed to retain,
all we couldn't hold
in grasping, clinging hands.
Let it bring its deep relief
to broken hearts
and tired limbs,
bruised and sore
though resilient still.

Standing firm,
though buffeted by winds.
Standing steady,
though unexpressed grief threatens.

Let the night fall.

Though so dark,
see the gift it brings.
Renewal,
rehabilitation, mercy,
restorative as the spring.
Spreading life anew
across our barren hearts;
planting seeds
of hope
and redemption.
While we thought
we were all done in,
night comes softly, reminding us
what 'sufficient for the day' means

Joy comes in the morning.

'Every morning tell Him, "Thank you for your kindness,"
and every evening rejoice in all His faithfulness.'

PSALM 92:2-4 (NIV)

Part 3:

LOVE

'We choose love by taking small steps of love every time there is an opportunity… Each step is like a candle burning in the night. It does not take the darkness away, but it guides us through the darkness. When we look back after many small steps of love, we will discover that we have made a long and beautiful journey.'

HENRI NOUWEN,
FROM 'BREAD FOR THE JOURNEY:
A DAYBOOK OF WISDOM AND FAITH'

Beauty Hunter

I am a beauty hunter.
Desiring to touch, taste and see.
To drink in sunsets,
run through waves,
chase the tail of the moon — and be free.

Beauty beckons to me,
as a siren call from the sea.
The only response to embrace -
nature, creation;
to stand in awe of its immensity,

and bow down before its beauty.

Except my heart, which was made for You
is restless in its search;
as it yearns to touch You,
strives to reach You,
with my worship for this earth.

Yet my soul, which expands,
so wide, with a view of the sea;
almost feels that heaven,
the essence of all creation, of all eternity,
has visited me

only, too briefly.

So what to do with a love, I said,
that can't do with only a fleeting smile,
a touch, or a view?
What to do with a passion,
a constant yearning for more?

This is what I heard Him say to me:
"This only do I seek -
that I may dwell in the house of the Lord
all the days of my life,
gaze on the beauty of the Lord

seek Him". And be free.

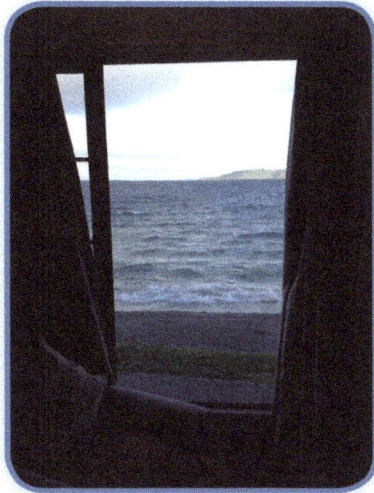

'However, the Most High does not live in houses made by
human hands. As the prophet says: "Heaven is My throne, and
the earth is My footstool. What kind of house will you build
for Me?" says the Lord. "Or where will My resting place be?
Has not My hand made all these things?"'
ACTS 7:48-50 (NIV)

Without Love

Without love,
who would I be?
It does more than cover a multitude of sins.

It puts up a mirror.
It shows me the self that, in Him I've always been.
The person whom, without love, I could never believe myself to be;

without His love reminding me,
of the beauty he sees in me.

Without love,
where would I be?
It does so much more than draw me home.

It provides a haven.
A place where I may lay it all down.
A place where my longings are at rest, and my restlessness tamed.

For love gives me a reason to return,
and a need to remain.

Without love,
why would I believe?
It does more than assure me of my right to be His.

It accepts and affirms me.
It seeks me relentlessly.
It says of me, "You are worthy beyond compare, and loved beyond belief."

And so love then becomes my reason,
and in response to Him, I become His gift.

Without love,
how can I live?
It does more than give me breath.

It takes my heart, from upside-down,
and turns it right around.
It takes my eyes, intently fixed, and instead turns them heaven-bound.

Until love then is all I see,
and in love I am found, and set free.

'You will be a crown of splendor in the Lord's hand, a royal
diadem in the hand of your God. No longer will they call
you Deserted, or name your land Desolate. But you will be
called Hephzibah, and your land Beulah, for the Lord will
take delight in you, and your land will be married. As a
young man marries a young woman, so will your Builder
marry you; as a bridegroom rejoices over his bride,
so will your God rejoice over you.'
ISAIAH 62:3-5 (NIV)

Come to Me

Come to me and love me,
like the sun rising.
Surprising in its warmth,
it's caress on my skin,
strengthening me within.
Like a plant stretching to the light,
make me want Your love,
and reach towards your heights.

Come to me and love me,
like the rain falling.
Gently refreshing,
soft upon my fields,
that I may lay there and yield.
Renewed as the parched earth,
make me need Your touch,
and fill my thirst.

Come to me and love me,
as the moon waxes full.
Held in its light,
reflecting silver rays,
unfolding under its gaze.
Smiling on my knees in tender reverence,
make me open to Your love,
in sweet surrender.

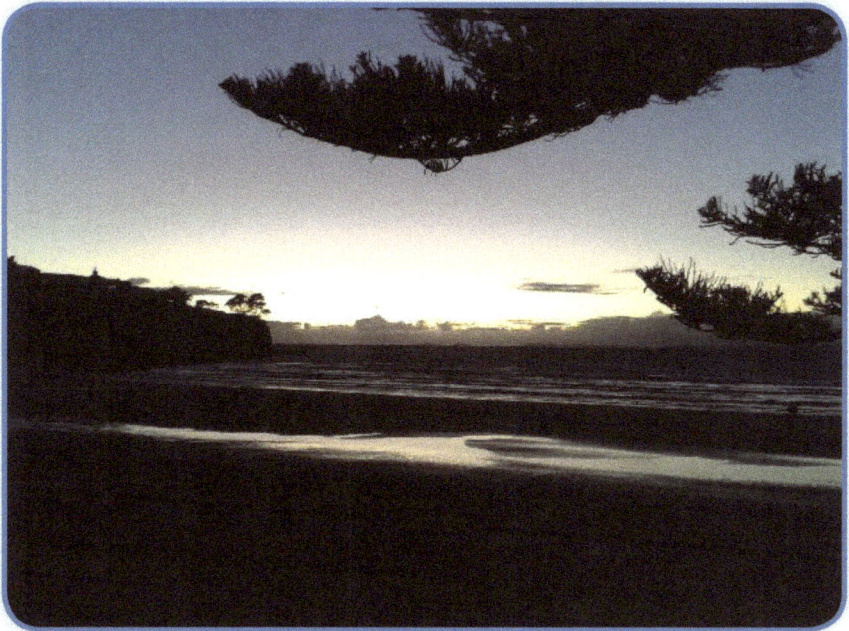

*'As the deer pants for streams of water, so
my soul pants for you, my God.
My soul thirsts for God, for the living God.
When can I go and meet with God?'*
PSALM 42:1-2 (NIV)

Lonely

'God puts the lonely in families'.
To me I understood it to be read, as;
'He finds a family for the lonely,
(if He wills it)',
but perhaps on reflection,
that's not all,
that was meant.

Perhaps as I sit here alone,
longing for a comforting arm,
aching for understanding;
maybe I've got it wrong?
Maybe loneliness is a given,
even in the midst of a family's bonds.

Maybe loneliness should be understood more,
as the catalyst for communion?
For if we are content in our family,
we wouldn't strive for union,
we wouldn't desire connection,
with the only One who can contain our longings.

And maybe loneliness is necessary,
to experience and appreciate,
another's human presence?
Maybe it's the dance of humanity,
to draw close and depart,
and maybe in the departure, we truly value the other's heart.

So it's okay to be lonely in my family,
because God has put me here.
And I know as close as I may feel tomorrow,
the next I'll feel far away.
But then I'll know my need for God,
and invite Him in to stay.

And though I may feel lonely in my family,
my family may feel so too.
And with a renewed appreciation of each other's worth,
we may build a bridge closer still.
Which although it may not hold with permanence,
we will daily rebuild.

'God sets the lonely in families, He leads out the prisoners
with singing; but the rebellious live in a sun-scorched land.'
PSALM 68:6 (NIV)

The Heart is a Wilderness

The heart is a wilderness
and the mind a map.
The heart would lose itself,
until the mind brings it back.

The heart is pure feeling,
and knows not time, or fact.
On a wave it will take you,
and won't let you forget.

The heart lives in a moment.
The mind looks forward and back.
The heart not knowing caution,
is, in its own emotions enrapt.

But the heart is a barometer.
The key to our innermost selves.
We know from what hurts, and what delights;
where our pain, and treasures lie.

The heart is a wild bird singing.
The mind its keeper and cage.
While the heart is passion aflame,
the mind is its necessary restraint.

Yes, the heart is a wilderness
and the mind a map.
The heart would lose itself,
until the mind brings it back.

'For the flesh desires what is contrary to the Spirit, and the
Spirit what is contrary to the flesh. They are in conflict with
each other, so that you are not to do whatever you want. But
if you are led by the Spirit, you are not under the law.'
GALATIANS 5:17-28 (NIV)

What Love

What love is this?
That would choose me,
that I might be His?
No indiscriminate,
indifferent,
'you will do'
selection,
made by Him;
but rather
a personal,
purposeful,
planned,
intentional
decision.

What love is this,
that would give,
up so much?
Fall so low,
as to take upon
Himself,
all our sin.
That would plan
to lose,
plan to give
up all,
so that we
by His humble offering,
might win.

What love is this?
And what is our response?
To a love that
didn't hesitate,
but rather knew
all along
the cost.
What is our response?
To Him,
who laid it all out;
His heart of love
for us,
in death
upon the cross.

What love is this?
Who died not only 'for' me,
but 'because' of me?
Because He wanted me,
longed for me,
sought me out
and fought for me.
Love that,
for all of us,
He would have done
what He did for us;
even if,
there were only
one of us.

What love is this?
A love we cannot
ignore,
cannot dismiss,
cannot fail to,
appreciate.
A love we must not
hesitate,
from embracing,
and celebrating.
Our gift to Him,
recognition,
of the true cost,
of our salvation.

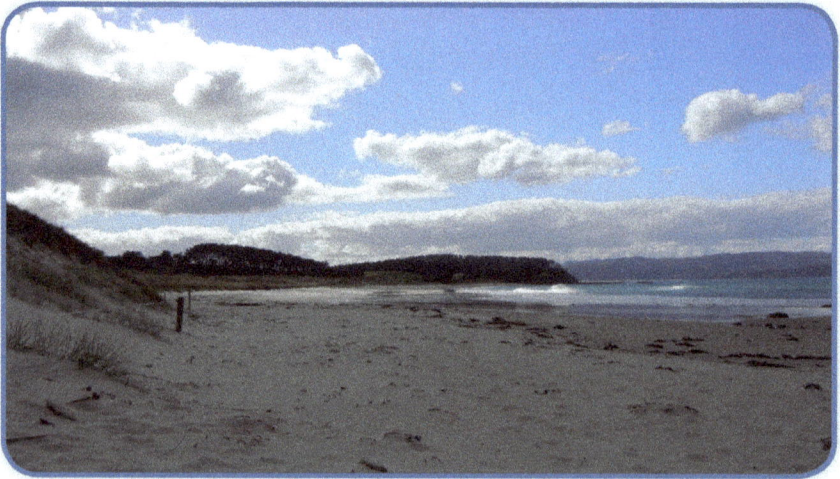

'*We have this hope as an anchor for the soul, firm and*
secure. It enters the inner sanctuary behind the curtain,
where our forerunner, Jesus, has entered on our behalf. He has
become a high priest forever, in the order of Melchizedek.'
HEBREWS 6:19-20 (NIV)

Cracks

I see you.
I see me.
Cracks running through our fragile hearts.
Sore places too tender to touch.
Walls too well defended to breach.
Hurts too well hidden to reach.

I see you.
I see me.
Cracks that will exist until they're accepted in us.
Sore places that will resist but the gentlest touch.
Walls that might melt if we're patient enough.
Hurts that may heal if given time, and love.

I see you.
I see me.
And the only way through, what defeats us,
is to love what is hardest to love.
To see with sympathy the unlovely parts.
To understand what is unconditional commitment.

That in the end it is the mortar and glue,
to our cracks, which with each hurt, expand and contract.
And might tear us apart, if not for love;
which in its magic unconditional touch,
loves in us,
what is ugliest.

'You, my brothers and sisters, were called to be free. But do
not use your freedom to indulge the flesh; rather, serve one
another humbly in love. For the entire law is fulfilled in keeping
this one command: "Love your neighbour as yourself."'

GALATIANS 5:13-15 (NIV)

Friendship

Friendship.
A chain of many links
that strengthens.
And with each gesture
and gift of self,
lengthens,
to become a chain of trust.
Not easily bought, or sold.
But made over long seasons
of developing, enduring love.

Friendship.
The result of
an exchange.
Disclosure met with acceptance,
a soft place to lay our heads,
and burdens down.
A warm room out of the rain.
A place to forget;
and to remember again,
what's truly important.

Friendship.
A mirror for
our best selves;
and gentle absolution
for our sins.
Reflecting our possibilities,
not focusing on our failings.

Showing us our light,
glowing with potential,
that we might shine it into being.

Friendship.
A starting place,
a finishing place;
and wayside in between.
A reminder, an encourager,
a place to rebuild
ourselves again.
An honest voice, and smile:
affirming, and restorative
as medicine.

Friendship.
A gift to give, and receive.
Mutual need, and mutual gain.

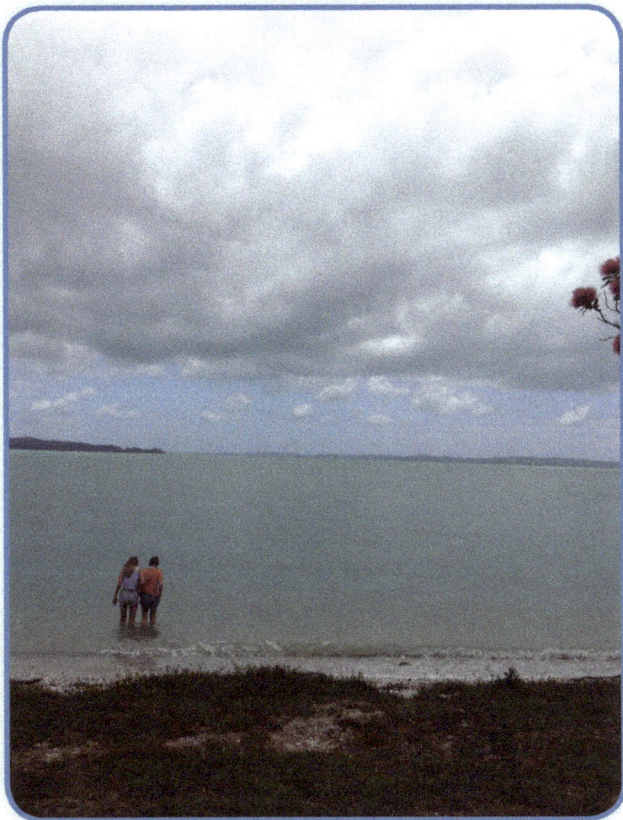

'...*Jonathan became one in spirit with David, and he loved him as himself.*'

1 SAMUEL 18:1 (NIV)

Joy is the Jewel

Joy is ours now.
After the rain has passed,
joy is the jewel
holding fast to the leaf,
moist as new born life,
shining in the light.

Joy is here now.
Knocking at your door,
joy is the friend's
embrace, claiming your right
to smile in return,
as you're reminded of your worth.

Joy is yours now.
Spread across the sky,
joy is the rainbow
that could not have been formed,
if not for the interplay
of light and dark, from passing storms.

Joy is right now.
Not forsaken, but found,
joy is the reminder
that we are never thirsty
for long, as surely as the earth
circles the sun, we drink from joy again.

*'The Spirit of the Sovereign Lord is on me... to comfort all
who mourn, and provide for those who grieve in Zion—
to bestow on them a crown of beauty instead of ashes, the
oil of joy instead of mourning, and a garment of praise
instead of a spirit of despair.'*

ISAIAH 61:1,3 (NIV)

Photo Appendix

Cover Photo: Stony Bay, Coromandel, New Zealand

Poetry Is Photo: Cathedral Cove Track, Coromandel, New Zealand

Introduction Photo: Fairy Falls, Waitakere Ranges, Auckland, New Zealand

Faith Comes Quietly Photo: Motuihe Island, Hauraki Gulf, Auckland, New Zealand

Light and Dark Photo: Upper Harbour, Whenuapai, West Auckland, New Zealand

Peace Photo: Whangamata Surf Beach, Coromandel, New Zealand

Hidden in Him Photo: Bethells Beach, Waitakere, Auckland, New Zealand

Thankful Photo: Matarangi Peninsula, Coromandel, New Zealand

Longing Photo: Upper Harbour, Whenuapai, West Auckland, New Zealand

Punishment Photo: Waikawau Bay, Coromandel, New Zealand

The River Photo: Upper Harbour, Whenuapai, West Auckland, New Zealand

Something New Photo: Whananaki North, Northland, New Zealand

Sunset Photo: Waikawau Bay, Coromandel, New Zealand

Arms of Grace Photo: Coromandel Peninsula, New Zealand

In Your Light Photo: Whangamata Surf Beach, Coromandel, New Zealand

In the Mirror Photo: Whitianga, Coromandel, New Zealand

To Lose Photo: Tawharanui, Warkworth, Auckland, New Zealand

Inside Photo: Whitianga, Coromandel, New Zealand

Wings Photo: Tawharanui, Warkworth, Auckland, New Zealand

Where there is Injury Photo: Long Bay, Auckland, New Zealand

Let the Night Fall Photo: Waiheke Island, Auckland, New Zealand

Beauty Hunter Photo: Taupo, New Zealand

Without Love Photo: Hauraki Gulf, Auckland, New Zealand

Come to Me Photo: Browns Bay, Auckland, New Zealand

Lonely Photo: Cathedral Cove Track, Coromandel, New Zealand

The Heart is a Wilderness Photo: Whangamata Surf Beach, Coromandel, New Zealand

What Love Photo: Tawharanui, Warkworth, Auckland, New Zealand

Cracks Photo: Little Bay, Coromandel, New Zealand

Friendship Photo: Waitawa Regional Park, Auckland, New Zealand

Joy is the Jewel: Hauraki Gulf, Auckland New Zealand

All photos are the author's own.

Acknowledgements

Excerpt from "A Home in Dark Grass" by Robert Bly, is reprinted from *Selected Poems*. Published by HarperCollins Publishers, 1986.

Excerpt from "Fireflies" by Rabindranath Tagore, is reprinted from *The English Writings of Rabindranath Tagore: Poems*. Edited by Sisir Kumar Das, 2004. First published in "The Visva-bharati Quarterly: Volume 4", 1926

Excerpt from "An Essay on Man" by Alexander Pope, is reprinted from *An Essay on Man*. Published by Pearson, 1965. First published 1734.

Quotation by Henri J.M. Nouwen, is reprinted from *Bread for the Journey: A Daybook of Wisdom and Faith*. Published by HarperOne, 1996.

www.ingramcontent.com/pod-product-compliance
Lightning Source LLC
Chambersburg PA
CBHW040312050426
42452CB00018B/2810